WILD
DELMARVA

Great Blue Heron

KEVIN FLEMING

Wild Delmarva was made possible by the generous support of NRG Energy,
the Delaware Department of Natural Resources and Environmental Control,
the Bank of Delmarva, and Delaware National Bank.

INTRODUCING WILD DELMARVA

Tom Horton
Tom Horton has written seven books focused on the Chesapeake Bay, including Turning the Tide: Saving the Chesapeake Bay and An Island Out of Time: A Memoir of Smith Island in the Chesapeake. Tom is a former environmental writer for the Baltimore Sun and he has also written for The New York Times Magazine, National Geographic and Rolling Stone.

What compels 20,000 Tundra Swans, among the world's largest and heaviest flighted birds, to journey 4,000 miles from breeding grounds across Alaska's North Slope and the Yukon Territories to winter on the Delmarva Peninsula?

What causes Horseshoe Crabs, living fossils little changed in more than 350 million years, to mass each May on Delmarva beaches in the greatest spawning concentration of the species anywhere in the world?

What draws half the East Coast's Striped Bass, which range from Maine to the Carolinas and can reach more than 80 pounds, back to Delmarva waters to release their eggs every spring?

The answer begins: Life loves an edge. Edges can be as intimate as the intersections of field and forest, upland and wetland or the place where shallows slope to channels. Special to Delmarva's wilder charms are the many edges of land and water.

Delmarva. Nowhere else in America does the sea intertwine so deeply and extensively with the land.

Delmarva Peninsula

On the peninsula's west lies the nation's greatest estuary, the Chesapeake Bay, which includes half a dozen major rivers and hundreds of tidal creeks. To the east lies the Delaware Bay, another estuary of national significance, with tens of thousands of acres of tidal marsh. And heading south, more than 100 miles of Atlantic barrier islands, coastal bays and ocean inlets are home to lush wetlands and underwater jungles of eelgrass.

Superficially, shrimp-shaped Delmarva is about 180 miles long and 488 miles around. But if you included all the meandering creeks, rivers, marsh guts and sloughs, the land-water edges would amount to several thousand miles.

Delmarva is also a relative island of solitude in the midst of the East Coast conurbation between Boston and Richmond. Its thousands of square miles of farm and forest remain lightly populated by humans, despite lying within a day's drive of tens of millions of Americans. To reach the heart of Delmarva by car, you must cross water. You can drive over a bridge that crosses the Chesapeake and Delaware Canal. Or you can take the Chesapeake Bay Bridge, the Chesapeake Bay Bridge-Tunnel or the Cape May-Lewes Ferry.

As birdwatchers from around the world know, Delmarva is positioned between two major funnels for migrating birds — Cape May to the east and the Kiptopeke-Cape Henry region at the peninsula's southern terminus. Everything from tiny warblers to Peregrine Falcons mass in both locations, awaiting favorable winds to make the jumps across the broad, lower portions of the Delaware and Chesapeake bays.

The most populous species on the peninsula (other than mosquitoes) is the domestic broiler chicken, of which more than half a billion are raised annually. While such intense meat production is not without environmental problems, the birds require a large amount of grain for feed, and the harvest leftovers on Delmarva's fields provide a significant source of winter food for various species, including swans, geese, White-tailed Deer and a range of smaller mammals, which in turn are food for hawks, owls and eagles.

These juxtapositions of edges, estuaries and open spaces make happy hunting grounds for photographer Kevin Fleming. He captures the heart and soul of Delmarva's nature, from Wild Turkey and snakes to turtles and seals; from Roseate Spoonbills to quail, beavers, skunks, foxes and raccoons. Kevin has long experience and uses the latest high-tech camera equipment; but just as important, he spends a lot of time in nature, watching and waiting, hours each day, every day there is decent light, year in, year out. It shows in the rarely seen behaviors documented in the book; moments in the lives of animals most people will not encounter in a lifetime.

It takes time and effort, and good knowledge of the peninsula's special places to discover the surprising range of nature in Wild Delmarva. Case in point: Kevin's photograph of a Great Blue Heron flying with a hapless Clapper Rail in its beak (following pages). Many people have seen a Great Blue statuesquely sentineling the margins of land and water, and many have seen them stab the shallows, coming up with a small fish, and assumed that's how they feed.

(Right) Great Egret • (Following pages) Great Blue Heron with Clapper Rail

But above all other wading birds, Great Blues also tackle large stuff, and they have been observed but seldom photographed killing and swallowing, anaconda-like, everything from adult muskrats and young kittens to yard-long snakes and fish that you'd be proud to have your picture taken with. Kevin was at the end of a long day in the marshes around Fenwick Island when, out of the corner of his eye, he spotted the heron around sunset, the struggling young rail firmly grasped in its marlinspike bill.

Royal Tern

"It was a lifetime shot," he recalls. As the sunlight faded, he clicked away as the Great Blue landed, strangled its prey and consumed it headfirst, a process that took about 10 minutes.

Birds and fish are not the only species that love the edges of land and water. Nationally, close to two thirds of Americans live on less than one fifth of the American landscape, in zones within 50 miles of the coastlines, including the Great Lakes.

Delmarva is no exception. Population here is growing rapidly, and sprawling suburbs have devoured more open space since the 1960s than in the preceding three and a half centuries since European settlement. Zoning and other controls on development are arguably fair to poor at best in most of the peninsula's 14 counties. Forests continue to decline, and drainage ditching for agriculture is a major and persistent source of stream and wetland degradation. Each year, dozens of miles of natural shoreline all over the peninsula are being bulkheaded and riprapped with boulders.

Still, you needn't travel far to enter Delmarva's wilder sides. Humans have protected enough extraordinary places here that we can celebrate all the wild that remains even as we lament all we've lost. A listing of the peninsula's special landscapes overlaps heavily with Kevin's favored haunts in shooting this book.

National wildlife refuges include Prime Hook and Bombay Hook on the Delaware Bay coast, which cover more than 26,000 acres, some 40 square miles. Blackwater National Wildlife Refuge in Maryland adds another 27,000 acres.

Assateague Island National Seashore in Maryland and Chincoteague Island National Wildlife Refuge in Virginia cover more than 60,000 acres of Atlantic beach, dunes, wetlands and coastal bays. Southward is the truly extraordinary Virginia Coast Reserve, nearly 70 miles of undeveloped Atlantic barrier islands and back bays that the private, nonprofit Nature Conservancy has protected for wildlife. A restoration of eelgrass there is the largest in the world.

Both Delaware and Maryland have enacted major protections for their coastal zones. Delaware, alarmed by signs in the late 1960s that industry would turn its bay coast into a Louisiana-style industrial and petrochemical complex, in 1971 passed the historic Coastal Zone Act prohibiting heavy industry in Delaware's 150-mile-long coastal zone.

Maryland's Coastal Program, established by executive order and approved in 1978, is a network of state laws and policies designed to protect coastal and marine resources. State protections from development also now cover permanently more than 100,000 acres of Delmarva farmland.

Delaware Wild Lands, a nonprofit, has helped preserve more than 50,000 acres of the peninsula's prime wildlife habitats, including remnants of the Great Cypress Swamp in Delaware. On the Maryland side of the peninsula, the Eastern Shore Land Conservancy has preserved an equal acreage. Add to this dozens of state and county parks, conservation easements by smaller local land trusts, and ongoing state conservation efforts — some of which have involved collaborations between multiple states.

The Chesapeake Bay Foundation, formed in 1967, puts a premium on maintaining natural lands throughout Delmarva as a way of filtering pollution runoff from agriculture and development before it reaches the waterways.

A promising new group, the Chesapeake Conservancy, recently secured passage of the nation's first all-water national park. The Captain John Smith National Historic Trail follows Smith's 1608 voyages of discovery around the Chesapeake, including his explorations into the heart of the peninsula to near modern-day Laurel, Delaware. The group, with state and federal cooperation, sees the water trail as a basis for major land preservation along Delmarva's edges.

What all this means to those willing to seek wild Delmarva goes beyond anything statistics can convey. It means it is possible to be literally caught in the midst of a massive spawn of striped bass, as I was a few years ago while kayaking a remote Delmarva marsh river. For nearly two hours, our boats were pressed, stem-to-stern, between 10- to 40-pound stripers, shoved this way and that, rudders thwacked by rolling fish. A paddle stuck down in the water 3 or 4 feet encountered solid fish.

It means that, as both Kevin and I have done many times, one can walk dozens of miles of Delaware Bay beach on a full moon night in May and watch spawning Horseshoe Crabs scrabble from the water until they pave the beach like cobblestones as far as the eye can see. Such evenings are ancient and elemental beyond any other experience of this earth: only moon and sand, the lap of

water and the scratch of shell on shell from creatures that were doing this when dinosaurs were still more than 100 million years in the future. It is the closest one can come to reentering primordial time. And if a giant military transport aircraft from Dover Air Force Base occasionally breaks the spell, well in some 400 million years, surely the old crabs have seen stranger sights.

It means that a band of paddlers entering Kegotank Bay near Gargatha Inlet in the Virginia part of Delmarva can watch a lone, bent waterman hurriedly picking up

Striped Bass

oysters from the exposed tide flats, just as Native Americans have done for centuries. The sun's setting kindles a glow across miles of green-golden salt marsh, tossing in a freshening sea breeze. Atlantic surf crashes on the outside of the inlet, mixed with the cry of migrating yellowlegs bound for Argentina. Later, we'll flag down the waterman as his skiff passes our campsite and pay 35 cents each for 100 of his choicest wild "salts," to be shucked and slurped, raw and roasted around the campfire.

Delmarva's touristy edges, such as Rehoboth Beach,

(Following pages) Red Fox kits

Delaware, and Ocean City, Maryland, will always be more famous than its little explored interior. But the latter has wild charm aplenty. It lies in the smaller, forest-canopied upper reaches of the broad rivers — Pocomoke, Wicomico, Nanticoke, Choptank and Chester — that drain the heart of the peninsula in both Maryland and Delaware. It also lies in the old millponds that dot the peninsula, little oases of nature amid the dominant grain fields and their ditched and straightened waterways. Here are rare Atlantic White Cedar, some huge old Bald Cypress, a

to rise faster than it has for thousands of years. This is abetted by land around Delmarva's edges subsiding. It is settling back to its contours from before the last advance of glaciers into Pennsylvania bulged up the land for hundreds of miles in front of the ice. The combination means it is likely that the peninsula will lose tens of thousands of acres of its tidal marshes and other low-lying lands within this century.

Within recorded history, Delmarva's lands have yielded an ever-changing bounty. Beavers, tobacco, wheat, fruit, vegetables and dairy were once major commodities. Now the prize commodities include chickens and the corn and soybeans grown to feed them. In the waters it's been a similar story of change. Sturgeon, Diamondback Terrapins and Oysters were once king. Now it's the Blue Crab. Kayakers, canoeists, jet skiers and pleasure boaters now dwarf the numbers of netters, tongers and potters in their workboats.

Yes, you can't stop change. But until recently, that change has mostly been a natural progression based on open landscapes and fertile soils, on relatively clean waters, accessible to all. Bulkheading shorelines and building developments near wetlands are more ominous changes. The same is true of paving over farmland and tattering unbroken forest habitat with new roadways and sprawling home sites.

The great edge of land and water that is Delmarva is itself on the edge, with pressure mounting to pave the landscape and armor the waterfront, to strike a so-called "balance" between humans and wildlife that always seems to shift in the same

Great Blue Herons

few approaching four centuries or more; also a stunning variety of amphibians, rare wetland plants, otter and beaver.

It is often said you can't stop Delmarva from changing — most often by those who would make a buck from developing the place. And, indeed, the very peninsula has not existed as such throughout most of geological time. Ice ages have shriveled the seas, locking them in glaciers. Chesapeake and Delaware bays once shrank to river gorges, and dry land extended 300 miles east of the present-day Rehoboth Beach and Ocean City.

In the nearer term, climate change is causing sea level

direction — more of us, less of the rest of nature. In the last several decades, we have developed more of Delmarva than in the preceding three and a half centuries since John Smith first charted the region in 1608.

Wild Delmarva can soon become a sad record of what existed; or it can become a basis for restoration and stewardship. The choice is ours. As we view Kevin's photographs and celebrate all that remains, we need to think hard about where nature and we are headed on this peninsula. And we need to act. Now. Because on much of the Delmarva Peninsula, there's still time to make better choices.

(Right) Great Blue Heron chick ⁕ (Following pages) Tundra Swan

NATURE IS A PHOTOGRAPHER'S BEST FRIEND.

As the sun rises over a Delmarva salt marsh, colors and light change by the minute, creating a spectacular beauty that's unique to every morning. No two days on the peninsula ever begin the same way. Some things, however, do not change. Everyday, wildlife engages in a life-or-death struggle. The predator must kill to prevent starvation. The prey seeks to stay alive. All animals and plants fight for survival against harsh elements.

The beauty and the battles all make nature a fascinating and fabulous subject.

For a year-and-a-half, my "office" has been outdoors in Delmarva's incredibly beautiful, wild places. From the hilly Piedmont in the north to the marshy southern tip of Cape Charles, and the streams, forests and fields in between, I have been fortunate enough to see and photograph an astonishing diversity of wildlife and wild places.

The hours were a little long, especially at the beginning of summer when the sun rises early and sets late. Usually, that's the best light of the day and the best time to see wildlife in action. After a night of hunkering down on a salt marsh or perching for hours in a tree, wildlife begins to stir at dawn. You have to be there early. Even just an hour after sunrise, the show is often over.

For this book, I used several Nikon D3S and D700 cameras with lenses ranging from a 14mm wide-angle to a long 600mm telephoto. Without a doubt, the 600mm is my favorite wildlife lens; it allows me to get close without disturbing wildlife.

People often ask me how long it took to take a certain photograph. That's a tough question to answer. Some of these images were shot within minutes of arriving at an island rookery or within seconds of setting up a long telephoto lens on a tripod near a feeding Great Blue Heron. On other occasions, it took many days to catch just the right moment, such as the photograph of the Snow Goose taking off with a mouthful of Winter cress (pages 62-63). I went out to photograph Snow Geese at least two dozen times and shot thousands of images in all kinds of weather and light. Only three photographs made the book, and I consider that a success. Sometimes, you have to go time and again to catch special moments like that.

I couldn't have done this book without the generous help of so many people, and I want to thank everyone who helped me along the way. I especially want to thank my wonderful fiancée, Susan McAnelly who has supported me and offered me many great ideas. My sons Jay and Ben are both outdoorsmen, and they helped me find and photograph some of the wildlife on these pages. My friend, Tony Pratt, joined me for many sunrise and sunset shoots. Having him there with his camera kept me on my toes. And I want to thank my assistant, Autumn Grinath, who expertly processed all of my photographs and traveled to China to supervise the printing of **Wild Delmarva**.

Tom Horton's foreword describes how Delmarva's geography is so unique in America and why the peninsula is so attractive for wildlife. Jim White's reptile chapter helps you find things that prefer not to be found. And I hope Derek Stoner's words inspire you to explore Assateague Island.

I asked Jeff Gordon to write a chapter on where and when you can find certain birds on Delmarva. He has written about some of my favorite spots, which appear in many of these photographs. If you take Jeff's advice, you will have a great time discovering birds and other wildlife on the peninsula.

This book was created to inspire you to discover and explore wild Delmarva and join in the battle for its conservation. Only people who love wildlife and wild places will fight to preserve and protect them. Environmental author Edward Abbey wrote, "God bless America. Let's save some of it." I say, let's start right here on the Delmarva Peninsula.

- Kevin Fleming

Wild Delmarva photographer Kevin Fleming on assignment

(Left) Glossy Ibis • Cattle Egret • (Following pages) Great Blue Herons and White Perch

"Never doubt that
a small group of
thoughtful,
committed citizens
can change
the world. Indeed,
it's the only thing
that ever has."

-- Margaret Mead

young Easten Cottontail
(Preceding pages) young Skunks

27

Mallard ducklings

"Plans to protect
air and water,
wilderness and

Canada Goose goslings

wildlife are in
fact plans to
protect man."

-Stewart Udall

"We simply need that wild country available to us, even if we never do more than drive to its edge and look in. For it can be a means of reassuring ourselves of our sanity as creatures, a part of the geography of hope."

-Wallace Stegner

nesting Black-backed Gulls

Black-backed Gull chicks

Discovering Delmarva's Birds
Ten field trips for great birdwatching

Jeffrey A. Gordon

Jeffrey A. Gordon is a tour leader and a frequent speaker at birding festivals all over North America. He writes for Bird Watcher's Digest and other publications and is the coordinator for the Delaware Birding Trail. His latest project is a series of video podcasts released in conjunction with the Peterson Field Guide to Birds of North America.

Herring Point, Cape Henlopean State Park

I'm often asked what I like best about birding on the Delmarva Peninsula, and I usually answer that it offers year-round action. Sure, birding in late January is generally less exciting — and less comfortable — than in mid-May, but there is something to interest birders here all year long.

Next on my list of Delmarva birding virtues is the diversity of habitat in a compact area. From steep-sided shady stream valleys in the north to sandy, storm-washed barrier islands in the south — with a wide array of forests and wetlands in between — Delmarva covers more biogeographical territory than its small size might suggest.

It takes a while to get a handle on the birding map and calendar. So I've put together a one-year itinerary of birding field trips. I trust that it will give you a good idea of why so many of us believe that Delmarva offers some of the best birding in North America.

Early March: Atlantic Beaches & Inlets, Maryland & Delaware

Use January and February to relax, leaf through a few field guides, and learn about the birds at your feeders. If you don't have birdfeeders, get some. Certainly, there are plenty of birds out and about to watch and enjoy in our coldest months, but I want our first trip to be memorable mostly for the birds and the scenery, not for the low temperatures.

Which isn't to say that a day at the beach in March is, well, a day at the beach. It can be bitterly cold. But you're welcome and even encouraged to choose a relatively mild day. Just remember that it will be colder by the ocean than anywhere inland.

Start at the north jetty of the inlet in Ocean City, Maryland, and work north, stopping at the south jetty of Delaware's Indian River Inlet and ending at Cape Henlopen

(Right) Bald Eagles • (Following pages) Ring-billed Gulls

State Park in Lewes. Or run it north to south, whichever is convenient. All these places offer two key commodities: a bay-ocean interface and rocks.

When the tide shoots in or out of the Ocean City or Indian River inlets, it creates a productive mix of waters. The same sort of thing happens in a larger and more diffuse way at Cape Henlopen, where the Delaware Bay meets the Atlantic Ocean. And in all three places, man has placed rocks in an attempt to guide the flow of water, calm the waves and break the less and less frequent ice.

The juxtaposition of rocks in the ocean makes for a locally rare and valuable habitat, mimicking in many ways the rugged coastlines farther north in New England and Atlantic Canada and attracting species typical of those regions.

These jetty and breakwater rocks attract a profusion of marine plant and animal life, including seaweed, barnacles, mussels and a host of more obscure comestibles for the wintering sea ducks and shorebirds, which are our main quarry today. Floating in the waters around the jetties, look for Scoters, chunky ducks cloaked in an abundance of velvety black feathers but with distinctive bill and head patterns. Black Scoters are most common, but a White-Winged is always possible.

Also watch for Long-tailed Ducks, svelte white-and-chocolate waterfowl, the drakes sporting their jaunty namesake tail plumes. There should also be a host of interesting duck-like divers: Common and Red-throated Loons, Horned Grebes and Double-crested and Great Cormorants.

Of course, you are likely to see a variety of gulls along the coast including Ring-billed Gulls and Herring Gulls.

On the jetties themselves — and please, watch your step as jetties are particularly slippery — you'll see a number of shorebirds. You may spot Ruddy Turnstones, Sanderlings and the occasional Dunlin, all of which you may have also seen in sandy habitats. Typically on the lowest, most treacherous, most spray-splashed crags are a few misleadingly named Purple Sandpipers. They almost entirely lack the violet hues one might imagine. Purple Sandpipers primarily winter in New England and along Canada's Atlantic coast. Here, we are seeing the species close to its southern limit.

On your way between Indian River Inlet and Cape Henlopen, take time for a quick stop at Silver Lake in the south end of Rehoboth Beach. There you should see a fine variety of waterfowl, including the annual flock of wild yet usually approachable Canvasbacks, surely one of the most elegant of all ducks.

Finally, if your winter beach trip falls in the second half of March, you may well encounter a Piping Plover or two, especially on the sands at Cape Henlopen. These tiny beach nesters typically return to our shores by St. Patrick's Day, though they won't actually nest for another month or so.

April: Pocomoke Cypress Swamps, Maryland

April can be a frustrating month on Delmarva. One expects mild, even warm weather. What one often gets is a baffling oscillation between sweltering heat and humidity straight out of July, followed by rapid descents into frigid temperatures that are a most unwelcome reminder of the winter thought to have just passed. In between, of course, are a few of those perfect spring days when all of life seems

Prairie Warbler

to be erupting like some great green pheromone-filled volcano. That's the time to head for the swamplands surrounding the main channel of the Pocomoke River.

Take a look at a satellite photograph of Delmarva. It's largely a nondescript agricultural-suburban khaki, with a generous garnish of scattered parsley-green forest. But down in the peninsula's middle, in a rough oval bounded by the towns of Frankford, Delaware, and Salisbury, Berlin and Pocomoke City, Maryland, you'll see that green coalesce into a relatively unbroken expanse of forest, by far the largest and most verdant in the entire region.

Darkest and greenest of all is the channel of the Pocomoke River itself, especially between Snow Hill and Pocomoke City. I recommend visiting at least Pocomoke River State Park and the Nature Conservancy's Paul Leifer Nature Trail at the historic site of Furnace Town. Pick a day in the latter half of April, when your taxes are filed or at least extended and the sun is shining. Stroll through the lovely bald cypress forest and piney uplands. And by all means, get out on the water. If you don't have

Prothonotary Warbler

your own watercraft, there are numerous opportunities to rent canoes and kayaks.

The Pocomoke and its forest attract a huge host of birds, especially the songbirds that migrate here to breed but spend the bulk of their year in the wilds of Central America. If the Pocomoke has a totem species, it's the Prothonotary Warbler. Although the bird was named to honor Catholic scribes — who donned yellow robes much as cardinals wore red ones — the moniker fails to convey the chromatic impact of the species. The colloquial name for the species, golden swamp canary, while taxonomically inaccurate, gets closer.

This bird is electric — it will shock your eyes. As vividly yellow-orange as a prize-winning tulip, with blue-gray wings, flashing white tail spots, a big dark eye and a lance of a bill, the males sing their ringing, "Sweet! Sweet! Sweet! Sweet! Sweet! Sweet! Sweet!" from cypress knees and sweet pepper bushes, their radiance reflected in the Pocomoke's dark tea waters.

A sight like this, I contend, is as restorative a springtime tonic as that first plate of local asparagus. You can feel the energy burning its way down inside your soul, thawing any last remnants of winter's long gray reign.

Of course, the Prothonotary is but one of the brighter stars in a brilliant constellation of birds here in late April. You may see Summer Tanagers and Indigo Buntings, each as pure a distillation of red and blue, respectively, as the Prothonotary is of gold. There is also a fine array of other warblers to be seen and heard, including Northern Parula, Prairie, Kentucky, Ovenbird, Hooded and Worm-eating.

Early May: White Clay Creek, Delaware

In April, the tide of spring migration is rising fast, but May is the month the levee breaks. So I have two assignments for you. The first, which you can do on just about any day between about May 5 and 15, is to go to White Clay Creek valley near Newark, Delaware. If you prefer, you can substitute White Clay with the valleys of the Brandywine River or Red Clay Creek, which are closer to the city of Wilmington. White Clay, however, is probably the most easily birded of the three.

An almost unimaginable variety of warblers and other migrants spill through these woods each spring. Given the right weather, you can find migrants just about anywhere on the peninsula, but these Piedmont woods are especially reliable. In May, we get our best crack at seeing many birds that wintered in Central or South America but will breed in New England or Canada or in the higher parts of the Appalachians. Many of species are only within Delmarva's borders for three or so weeks in May and then again for a few more weeks in late summer and early autumn. That's it. If you want to see them here, that's when you go out.

Spring has a couple of advantages over fall. The birds tend to look their most colorful and distinctive as they prepare to attract mates and repel rivals. At the same time, they are also very vocal, making it easier to locate them even if you're not entirely sure of the singer's identity.

It's a truly thrilling thing to follow a song issuing from a treetop or thicket and be rewarded with a glimpse of a Rose-breasted Grosbeak, a Blue-headed Bireo, or any of a myriad of warblers: Canada, Black-throated Blue, Blackburnian or a dozen others.

Late May: Slaughter Beach, Delaware

Our second May trip is the most unusual of the year and also the most globally significant — a pilgrimage to the shores of Delaware Bay for the annual Horseshoe Crab spawn and attendant shorebird migration.

Horseshoe Crabs aren't birds, of course. More surprisingly, they're not even crabs. The Horseshoe Crab is an ancient sea-dwelling arachnid. But don't let images of giant underwater spiders put you off. Horseshoe Crabs, despite their rather fearsome appearance, are the epitome of harmlessness. They don't bite, they don't pinch, and they don't sting. At this time of year, they are primarily about breeding.

For Horseshoe Crabs, reproduction is anything but a romantic, private affair. Each high tide, especially at night and when the tide is heightened by the pull of a full or new moon, thousands of these creatures crawl out of the depths of the bay, creating a bizarre prehistoric traffic jam along the water's edge. The larger females are intent on reaching a suitably high but not completely dry patch of sand, where they will dig down and deposit thousands of gray-green eggs masses.

Some will attempt this in April, others in June, but traditionally, late May is the time when the largest numbers cast their lots. As the females make their amphibious march, they are beset by males, each jockeying for position, clamping firmly to the female's shell, if possible, so that they can fertilize the eggs that the female deposits.

This system, while effective, is not what you'd call efficient. Millions of eggs wash out before they have a chance to hatch. Even a perfectly located nest may be dug up and destroyed by the breeding activities of subsequent females. So there's an awful lot of protein along the beach. Enter the shorebirds.

In late April and early May, we see some impressive migrants, birds that might spend October through March in, say, Honduras or Panama, then make the trek to Delmarva for April into September. It's a grand journey, to be sure. But look at the itinerary of a Red Knot, who

spends the winter much farther south, perhaps all the way in Tierra del Fuego, then works its way up the Atlantic Coast of South America. The Red Knots make a punishing ocean crossing to Delaware Bay then pushes on to their remote Arctic breeding grounds in northern Canada. Now that's a migration. And the stop at Delaware Bay turns out to be a crucial one.

The Red Knot arrives here famished, its carefully acquired fat reserves depleted. It must replace that rich pad of migration fuel if it is to successfully complete its journey and arrive in the peak condition necessary to undertake

Yellow-rumped Warbler

(Following pages) Great Blue Herons

the rigors of breeding. Horseshoe Crab eggs are the vital link that allows the Red Knot (following pages) to accomplish this metabolic trapeze act. If the eggs aren't there in sufficient quantity, the show's over.

The amount of time it takes the knots and other shorebirds to refuel and press on each year varies, according to a complex equation involving weather, water temperature and the moon phase — and that's just to start. To have the best chance of seeing both

reveal the results of the latest spawning. At mid and low tides, there is so much mudflat exposed that the action can be a bit dispersed.

Remember, be cautious when you approach feeding birds. Go slow and stay low, and you will be rewarded with good views. If the birds are moving away from you, especially if they flush, back off — you're too close and they have work to do.

Whether in the woods or on the beach it's the fleeting nature of these spring spectacles that makes them so precious. The energy and excitement is palpably at its peak, but that massive wave will soon crest, break and be gone. Birders wait all year for May. I urge you not to miss out.

June: Smith Island, Maryland/Virginia

The salt marshes and sandy islets that ring Delmarva are our wildest and most ecologically valuable habitats. In contrast to the well-trodden core, our watery, muddy fringes tend to be difficult to access and, despite many attempts at development and exploitation, to retain a largely wild character.

The scattering of islands in Chesapeake Bay astride the Maryland-Virginia line are arguably the most remote places in the region, yet it's relatively easy to visit Smith Island — and you should. Catch the ferry from Crisfield, Maryland or from Point Lookout on Maryland's Western shore. Bring your own canoe or kayak, if you have one — the ferryman is used to that. Plan to stay overnight at

Pine Warbler

shorebirds and Horseshoe Crabs, I recommend visiting Slaughter Beach around the third week of May, though that might slip a day or two earlier or later in the direction of the new or full moon. Yes, this is your most time critical assignment. If in doubt, go a little early. Go too late, and the birds may be largely or wholly gone.

Start at the DuPont Nature Center at the north end of Slaughter Beach. Make sure that you visit the actual bayshore, too. Arriving at or near high tide will usually result in the closest and most dramatic views of both birds and crabs, as the watery curtain is drawn back to

one the public accommodations in Tylerton or Ewell — just be sure to make reservations first.

At Smith Island, which is actually a group of islets, you'll find three tiny communities totaling only a few hundred residents. There's a nice museum in Ewell, the Smith Island Center, and you can walk the mile-long road from there to tiny Rhodes Point, which goes past a lovely stretch of marsh that is usually bursting with herons, egrets, ibis, clapper rails and seaside sparrows. Tylerton, too, is a nice place for a casual stroll around town.

To really see Smith Island, though, you're going to have to get back on the water. If you brought your own boat, there are miles of well-marked water trails. If you're boat-less, it's usually not at all difficult or expensive to hire one of the local watermen to take you on a birding expedition. Even veteran paddlers may want to do this, as it offers a great chance to learn about the area from those who know it best.

As you cruise through the creeks and guts that dissect the islands, you'll see a fabulous variety of large wading birds. Just about all our herons are to be found here, as are terns, gulls, skimmers and Oystercatchers. There is also a spectacular Brown Pelican and Double-crested Cormorant rookery across the Virginia line in the southern reaches of Smith Island.

When visiting any of these areas, it's critically important to be aware of how the birds are responding to you. Flushing parents away from their nests can quickly — in a matter of minutes — lead to the loss of eggs and chicks to exposure or predators. Moreover, much of the land here and all of the birds are federally protected. If you're unsure about access, stay back.

Life has a tenuous quality on Smith Island that makes simply surviving seem a beautiful triumph. There's the constant threat of damaging storms (less so in June), and in recent decades, a rise in sea level and increased erosion have literally eaten away much of the ground on which the islanders, both human and avian, depend. But for all that, there's a feeling of being free from time, too, of stepping back into a slower, more deliberate era. It's an experience not to be missed.

August: Bombay Hook and Prime Hook, Delaware

I'll be honest with you here — this trip isn't for everybody. In early August, seemingly everybody is at the beach. It's cooler there, the air is fresh and there's usually a nice breeze. In the marshlands along Delaware Bay, it's hot and muddy and muggy and buggy. It's not everybody's cup of tea.

But you're not everybody. You're willing to put up with a little discomfort in order to see the best of the peninsula's birdlife, right? So here's a deal: Give me the morning along the mudflats and in the afternoon, we can all head to the beach for a nice dip. How's that?

I promise you there will be plenty of birds. For us, it's the zenith of summer. For many of them, it's well into

Brown-headed Nuthatch

autumn. Most shorebirds have started back from the Arctic, the vanguard having reached us in early July. By the beginning of August, the southward tide is already in flood. The herons and egrets have fledged their young, and they concentrate, sometimes by the hundreds, around drying pools that temporarily offer easy fishing.

I'm going to leave the itinerary this month somewhat open. Suffice it to say that you're likely to find great birding anywhere along Bombay Hook National Wildlife Refuge's auto tour route or on the coastal impoundments along Fowler Beach, Prime Hook Beach

Red Knot • (Preceding pages) Red Knot • (Following pages) Horseshoe Crabs

and Broadkill Beach roads in Prime Hook National Wildlife Refuge. It's also true that these are some of North America's better birding spots in any season, so you should go there at other times, too.

Summer can be an especially good time to avail yourself of the wealth of up-to-the-minute local birding information, available from refuge visitor centers and on the Internet. There are a variety of websites and mailing lists on which birders freely share their latest sightings. Since the best summer shorebirding is so dependent on local and changing water levels, and since this is the prime season for stray species from as far away as Europe and Asia to turn up locally, it's very helpful to have good scouting information. You might even join a bird club or nature center-sponsored field trip, as shorebirds are at times notoriously vexing to identify and there's simply no substitute for spending time afield with others who are further up the learning curve.

September: Chincoteague, Virginia

In September, birding is good just about anywhere on Delmarva, and at Chincoteague, Virginia, birding is good to excellent any day of the year. So you're heading for one of our best birding spots at one of our best birding times — an unbeatable combination. Just promise me you won't neglect other great birding spots in September and that you'll go to Chincoteague in other seasons as well. (The Maryland part of this barrier island is called Assateague.)

The heart of the birding here is the Wildlife Loop, 3.2 miles of road that runs through prime wetlands. Access here operates on a unique schedule. From an hour before sunrise until 3 p.m., the road is open to pedestrians and bicyclists but not cars. From 3 p.m. until an hour after sunset, cars may also traverse the road. So plan your visit accordingly — come early if you want to enjoy a self-powered, low-carbon experience. If the day is hot or the insects are many, you may wish to schedule an afternoon trip.

The impoundments along the loop road offer similar birding to that found at Bombay Hook and Prime Hook; the area is heavy on the waterbirds and shorebirds that are Delmarva's signature. But watch the bushes and forest edges, too. September is the biggest month for songbirds heading south, and it's a last chance to intersect with a lot of those boreal breeders that blew through so quickly in May. True, many are in rather drab plumages and almost nobody is singing, but the sheer numbers of birds can be impressive. Remember, for every two adults that flew north in the spring, the hope is that there is a whole clutch of youngsters finding their way south in fall.

Don't forget the marshes along the causeway from the mainland and the ocean beaches. As always, increasing the number of habitats you visit will result in a longer and more varied bird list. Chincoteague is also an excellent place to see mammals, from native deer to dolphins to introduced ponies and Sika Elk.

Brown Pelican (Above and following four pages) • (Preceding pages) Gulls, Willets, knots, sandpipers and turnstones feast on Horseshoe Crab eggs.

Keep a careful eye out for the endangered Delmarva Fox Squirrel, brought to the refuge in 1968 in an attempt to establish an additional, well-protected population of this imperiled animal.

October: Kiptopeke, Virginia

The Delmarva Peninsula has an interesting elongate shape. If you squint a little and use your imagination, it might resemble a seahorse. At the tip of that seahorse's tail is Kiptopeke, and in fall, it is the narrow opening at the end of a very large funnel. Just like a funnel collects and concentrates whatever is poured into it,

Delmarva's shape collects and concentrates southbound birds.

Most birds, especially diurnal, terrestrial migrants like hawks, are loath to cross much water. They'll go a good bit out of their way to stay over land, so once they're on Delmarva, chances are good they're heading for Kiptopeke. Even species that are untroubled by over-water flights, such as Peregrine Falcons or Merlins, will often follow coastlines when it's efficient.

By placing ourselves right at the mouth of this giant migration bottleneck, it is often possible to see huge concentrations of common species and large numbers of scarcer ones. Even rarities

become — in relative terms — frequent. And the effect applies not only to raptors but songbirds, shorebirds, even butterflies and dragonflies. It's harvest season, and the basket is full.

All nature observation is influenced by weather, but this is probably our most meteorologically complicated trip of the year. What we want is for a storm front to pass, leaving colder northwest winds in its wake and sunny to partly cloudy skies. Winds from that direction push migrant birds south and toward the coast, where Kiptopeke serves

Grasshopper Sparrow

as a funnel. Such cycles typically happen every week or so in October. So if you can, time your visit for the day or two just after a rainy low-pressure system passes. If circumstances force you to visit on a warm Indian summer day with breezes out of the south, you may leave a bit disappointed, wondering what all the hype is about.

The key spots to hit are the hawk watch and the banding stations at Kiptopeke State Park and the visitor center at the Eastern Shore of Virginia National Wildlife Refuge. At the hawk watch, you can witness the biggest flights of raptors anywhere on Delmarva and benefit from the experts, who can help identify what you see. The banding station is unusually accessible to visitors and

offers an unparalleled chance to see birds close up as they are fitted with numbered bands in an effort to better document and understand their migration. The refuge visitor center can point you in the direction of a number of fine birding spots; it's also surrounded by an extensive butterfly garden.

November: Blackwater National Wildlife Refuge, Cambridge, Maryland

Autumn is traditionally the season of abundance, and in November, Delmarva birding reaches a thundering climax as the noisy hordes of waterfowl that we last saw in March or early April return to our shores, their numbers now swollen with the young of the year. The masses of geese, ducks and tundra swans that descend upon us inspire awe in even the most reluctant birdwatcher, who could never be bothered to appreciate the subtle beauty of sparrows or flycatchers. If you like your birds big, loud and out in the open, then November is your month.

Once again, Delmarva is blessed with an embarrassment of riches, and there are a number of first-rate spots where you can view these waves of waterfowl. But I've chosen Blackwater National Wildlife Refuge near Cambridge, Maryland, because the marshes of the Eastern Shore have such a storied history in waterfowl hunting and conservation.

I'll admit, some of the goose chases I've sent you on have been a little tricky, but this one's easy. Go in the sun, go in the rain, in the morning, in the afternoon — there will always be something to see. Better still, stay long enough to experience the phenomenon in a variety of weather and lighting conditions. And don't neglect the birds without webbed toes. Blackwater is especially famous for hosting large numbers of Bald Eagles and the even more rare Golden Eagle. It's also great for seeing smaller birds like sparrows, which are at their peak of migration in late October and early November.

But mostly, just let the sounds and sights and the majesty of this annual cycle wash over you. Winter is coming, but it's not here yet. Enjoy.

Late December/early January: Christmas Counts, Delmarva-wide

Birding certainly can be a solitary activity. Many of its lessons are learned when one is alone, without others to provide quick answers to queries. But the real strength of birding is in its community. Seeing what a dedicated group of people can accomplish when they work together is one of the distinct pleasures of life. This month, as a

(Right) Horned Lark   •   (Following pages) Snow Goose

way of closing out our year of exploring Delmarva's birds, I'm challenging you to become part of that community.

The Christmas Bird Count, first conducted in 1900, has become birding's biggest annual citizen science effort. Organized around 15-mile radius circles, the count provides an annual look at winter bird population trends and has become one of the most valuable data sets we have.

But you wouldn't necessarily guess that from ground level. Christmas Counts, for most of us, are a big excuse to get together, see a bunch of birds, tell a lot of stories and generally have fun. Yes, it's a bit more structured than just going off birding on one's own, but it's an amazing chance to be part of a larger effort — and to learn and to have fun.

There are Christmas Count circles all over Delmarva. Choose one that includes your favorite birding area, one you haven't visited yet or, perhaps best of all, one near your home. The counts occur on pre-arranged dates, somewhere between December 14 and January 5. Each count has a compiler, whom you can usually find with just a bit of Internet searching. Contact him or her, preferably a week or two before the count date, and tell them you'd like to help out. They'll let you know which areas and/or parties can use help. Don't worry if you can only spare a few hours. Chances are there's a way to put you to use.

Be sure to ask if there's a tally rally — a session during which birders gather at day's end to share the day's sightings. Not only is it a great opportunity to share your hits and misses for the day, but it's also a wonderful place to hear about other favored birding spots, field trips and activities that will keep you busy and birding Delmarva for years to come.

A few resources

This has been a very quick overview of the endless opportunities to see and enjoy birds here. Both Virginia and Delaware have excellent birding trail guides available online, and Maryland is likely to follow soon. These guides offer the best summary advice for birding and bird finding. For more detailed information, your best bet is to contact bird clubs like the Delmarva Ornithological Society, the Maryland Ornithological Society and the Virginia Society of Ornithology. There are also numerous visitor centers, nature centers and park and refuge offices. Audubon chapters, most of which have their own websites, usually have staff or volunteers who can answer questions and offer you lots of invaluable help in planning your birding trips. Just search around a little bit, or ask those other birders you see in the field. We're generally very happy to share. Good birding!

Snow Geese (Left and following pages)

There is a pleasure in
the pathless woods,
There is a rapture on
the lonely shore,
There is society,
where none intrudes,
By the deep sea, and
music in its roar:
I love not man the
less, but Nature more.

-Lord Byron

White-tailed Deer fawns

(Left) White-tailed Deer doe · White-tailed Deer buck

young White-tailed Deer bucks

"We abuse land
because we regard
it as a commodity
belonging to us.
When we see land
as a community to
which we belong,
we may begin to
use it with love
and respect."

-Aldo Leopold

North American Beaver • (Following pages) Snow Geese at dawn over the Delaware Bay

"We cannot win this battle to save species and environments without forging an emotional bond between ourselves and nature as well - for we will not fight to save what we do not love."

-Stephen Jay Gould

"Wild beasts and
birds are by right not
the property merely
of the people who are
alive today, but the
property of unknown
generations, whose
belongings we have
no right to squander."

-Theodore Roosevelt

Great Egrets • (Preceding pages) Lewes,
Delaware harbor clogged with ice

nesting Great Egret • (Following pages) Eastern Tiger Swallowtail

"If people destroy
something
replaceable made
by mankind, they
are called vandals;
if they destroy
something
irreplaceable made
by God, they are
called developers."

-Joseph Wood Krutch

"We crush all the
caterpillars, then

Hummingbird Moth

complain there are

no butterflies."

-author unknown

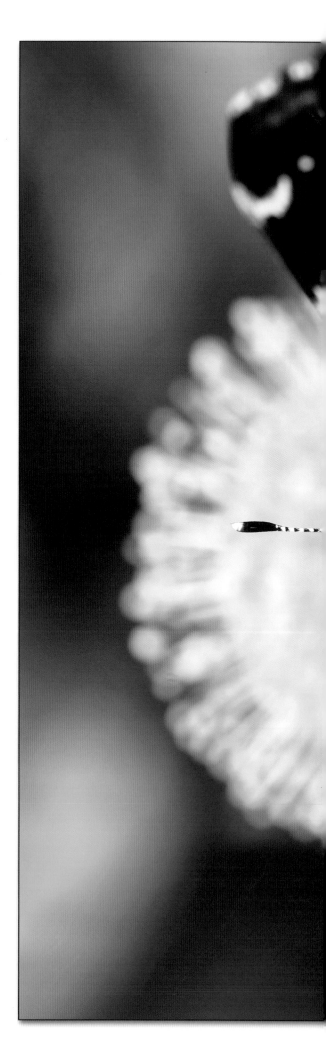

Red Admiral

Hover Fly

"Teaching a child not to step on a caterpillar is as valuable to the child as it is to the caterpillar."

-Bradley Miller

Hibiscus Bee   •   (Right) Honey Bees   •   (Following pages) Roseate Spoonbill

(Left and above) Bald Eagles at dawn • (Preceding pages) Bald Eagle with Walleye

"The quicker we humans learn that saving open space and wildlife is critical to our welfare and quality of life, maybe we will start thinking of doing something about it."

-Jim Fowler

Barred Owl with young songbird
(Following pages) Osprey

HOW NOT TO BE SEEN:
The Secret Lives of Amphibians and Reptiles

Jim White

Jim White is a native Delawarean, with more than 30 years of experience studying and teaching about the state's amphibians and reptiles. He is co-author, with his wife Amy, of Amphibians and Reptiles of Delmarva, a 250-page field guide to the 70 amphibian and reptile species known to occur on the Delmarva Peninsula. He is currently associate director for land and biodiversity management at the Delaware Nature Society.

Wildlife watching is one of the most common nature activities. Bird watching, today just called "birding," seems to gain popularity with each passing year. Butterfly watching is also one of nature enthusiasts' favorite activities, and, more recently, many nature-minded folks have become obsessed with observing

and identifying odonates (damselflies and dragonflies). So why does amphibian and reptile watching, known as "herping," lag so far behind in popularity? Well, you may say it's because no one likes them, and you may have a valid point for one group: snakes. But who doesn't like frogs,

salamanders, turtles and lizards? And surely the behavior of herpetiles is equally if not more interesting than the behavior of many groups of well-watched animals. Moreover, the physical appearance of herpetiles rivals that of any other animal group in uniqueness.

I believe that the reason why so few people pursue amphibians and reptiles is that most herpetile species are secretive and remain out of human sight. Unlike the majority of birds — and all butterflies and odonates — many herpetiles are nocturnal, and even those that are active during the day often move under the cover of rocks, soil, debris, vegetation or water. Also, many herpetiles live in areas that humans do not frequently visit, such as temporary wetlands, swamps and marshes. However, for the few of us who do enjoy herping, the knowledge of their secretive lives is the key to finding and observing these amazing creatures.

In general, a nocturnal life is a secretive life, at least from the human perspective. Humans are ill-adapted to the night. Not only do we see poorly in the dark, but we also follow a daily biological clock (i.e., circadian cycle) that usually prevents us from being active too long after sunset. In addition, it is fairly common for humans to be somewhat fearful of the dark. Many herpetiles, on the other hand, thrive at night, actively feeding and reproducing under the cover of darkness. Frogs are a good example. The vast majority of frog species on the Delmarva Peninsula reach their peak activity level after dark. The relative coolness and high humidity of spring and summer nights create ideal conditions for these amphibians. On a warm night in late spring, you are likely to find amazing congregations of breeding frogs. Vernal wetlands throughout the peninsula come alive with the trills, clucks, chuckles, snores, grunts, chirps, growls, barks and other loud calls made by male frogs. On a good night in some of our vernal wetlands, called "Delmarva Bays," the Eastern Cricket Frog, Gray Treefrog, Cope's Gray Treefrog, Southern Leopard Frog, Northern Green Frog, American Bullfrog and even the rare Barking Treefrog call together, creating a truly amazing cacophony of sound. It is an adventure indeed to visit one of these wetlands during the spring and wade out into the middle of the dark water to experience this musical breeding frenzy.

The Lungless Salamanders (Family Plethodontidae) is another group of herpetiles that live most of their lives out of human sight. Species like the Northern Dusky Salamander, Northern Red Salamander and Northern Two-lined

Eastern Box Turtle • (Right and following pages) Snapping Turtle

Salamander spend much of their time in cool spring-fed creeks. These salamanders are also primarily nocturnal, and you are unlikely to observe them unless you are inclined to either wade in ankle-deep creeks, while bending down to turn over the rocks and logs under which they hide during the day; or walk along country roads near creeks on rainy spring and summer nights, when these slippery little salamanders can be found out in the open crossing the roads.

Another Lungless Salamander species that restricts

Five-lined
Skink

most of its activity to the night is the Long-tailed Salamander. Typically, this species comes out into the open only on humid or rainy nights to forage for food. In addition to being hidden from humans by the dark of night, this brightly colored salamander spends much of the fall, winter and early spring underground in the rocky crevices of spring seeps. This subterranean habitat provides this species with a moist and relatively constant temperature in which to spend the coldest months. However, the Long-tailed Salamander is not hibernating in the rocky springs but instead may be very active in the underground crevices. Nathan

Nazdrowicz of the University of Delaware studied this species of secretive salamander for six years and found that Long-tailed Salamanders mate and lay their eggs underground in the cool rocky springs in late fall and early winter. The eggs develop slowly over the winter and hatch in early spring. Three to four months later, the larvae swim out into the small stream into which the spring flows.

While many herpetiles are nocturnal, there are some species that are most active during the day, yet they still manage to stay out of our sight. The Bog Turtle is one of these animals. This diminutive turtle is one of the least encountered of Delmarva's herpetiles for several reasons. For one, they are found only in freshwater marshes or bogs, a habitat that humans don't frequent. For another, they are compulsive burrowers, spending much of their time tunneling under the mud and vegetation. Even when these turtles bask in the sunlight to raise their body temperatures to optimal levels, they don't climb up on logs or rocks like other aquatic turtles. Instead, the Bog Turtle basks by lying on the bog surface or on top of low vegetation, making it very difficult to observe them. Still another reason why humans rarely see the Bog Turtle is that it is one of the most rare herpetiles on Delmarva, due largely to the loss of suitable habitat. In fact, this turtle is rare throughout its range in eastern North American, and the federal government has put it on the list of threatened species. (It is the only Delmarva herpetile on the list.) The pet trade has also contributed to the decline in Bog Turtle populations. A live Bog Turtle can be worth hundreds of dollars. Hopefully, their federally protected status, along with their secretive lifestyle, will help conserve these incredible little turtles.

Among Delmarva's most recognizable herpetiles species, the Eastern Box Turtle is fairly common in woodlands and associated meadows throughout much of the eastern United States. The adult turtles, which are often diurnal, are not particularly secretive. It is not uncommon to encounter one crawling across an open area such as a lawn, a trail or, unfortunately, a roadway. However, the vast majority of observed Box Turtles are adults, usually over 15 years old and sometimes much older. It is rare indeed that young Box Turtles are found in the open. It seems that juveniles are very secretive and spend much of the time burrowed under leaves or loose soil. This secretiveness serves them well, as young turtles would make a tasty meal for such mammals as raccoons, opossums and fox. As Box Turtles mature and reach full size (about 5 to 6 inches long) they are much less vulnerable to predation, which may allow them to become less secretive. Their ability to close their hard carapace (top shell) and plastron (bottom shell) together like a box protects the adult turtle's soft body from most predators' claws and teeth. Unfortunately, their hard shells do not protect them from automobile drivers who are not paying attention to the roadway ahead.

Some kinds of snakes are also observed rather frequently, much to the chagrin of more than a few folks. You may find the Eastern Gartersnake, Common Watersnake, Northern Black Racer and Eastern Ratsnake coiled up in a brush pile, slithering across lawns and gardens, or climbing shrubs and trees. However, most snakes shun open spaces, and several are rarely found anywhere but under logs, rocks or debris. Humans rarely encounter these snakes, even if they are looking for them. One such snake is the small Northern Red-bellied Snake, which is less than 10 inches long. These snakes are a rare find even for the most tenacious herper. Feeding on slugs and worms, the snake finds much of its prey under the very cover where it prefers to live. Although it would make any

Delmarva herper's day to find a Northern Red-bellied Snake, he or she would not be overly impressed by its initial appearance. The coloration of the back and sides is a rather unexciting brown. In contrast, the snake's belly scales are bright orange to red, colors that often signal danger in the animal world. This species of snake may use its belly coloration to fool predators into thinking it is poisonous or otherwise unpalatable.

Many herpetile species use another approach to remaining unseen: camouflage. These species rely on

Eastern American Toad

blending into the background for protection. Frogs are often hard to see because their skin coloration can be similar to the surface that they are on. Green Treefrogs are a good example. Their bright green color often matches the green leaves of the plant to which they are clinging. Eastern Cricket Frogs also blend well into the dark, often algae-covered surface of the muddy pond edges that they frequent; this species is so good at hiding "in plain sight" that even experienced eyes have a hard time seeing them unless they move. In fact, even common, larger species such as the American Bullfrog and Northern Green Frog can be difficult to see as they

(Following pages) Long-tailed Salamander

Red-bellied Snake • (Right) Spotted Salamander • (Following pages) Copperhead

sit motionless along the edges of ponds. When walking around the perimeter of ponds or along creeks in mid-summer, it's hard not to be startled by these frogs. They seem to come out of nowhere and noisily jump out from under our feet to the safety of the water.

But the prize for the best camouflage among Delmarva's herpetile species, in my opinion, goes to the Copperhead. This snake's back color and pattern seem to blend into a variety of backgrounds. Whether they are near rocks, leaves or sandy soil, Copperheads are difficult to spot. I found a Copperhead and, after briefly taking my eye off of it to adjust my camera, had trouble seeing it, even though it had not moved. The Copperhead's camouflage not only protects it from predators, but it also helps the snake to obtain its prey. The Copperhead is what is called a "sit-and-wait predator." The snake finds a suitable location to curl up and wait for a mouse or other warm-blooded animal to pass it. When the unsuspecting creature walks close enough, the snake strikes, injecting its deadly venom. Although the mouse usually can run away, it is doomed. The venom will soon immobilize and kill the mouse. Using its heat-sensing pit, the Copperhead tracks the heat trail left by the mouse until it finds and ingests its dead prey. Fortunately for humans who like to spend time outdoors, Copperheads are relatively docile and rarely bite unless handled.

There are some reptiles that have yet another trick up their scales to help them remain unseen by most humans: speed. And when it comes to speed, lizards are the drag racers of the herpetile world. Lizards such as the Common Five-lined Skink and Broad-headed Skink often dart out of sight so fast that it is difficult to determine what kind of animal was actually there. Another speedster is the diminutive Little Brown Skink, which spends most of its life on the forest floor searching for the tiny invertebrates on which it feeds. Many times while walking down a woodland path, I have been alerted to something scampering in the leaves, only to have the lizard elude me with its blinding quickness.

While field herping may never become as popular as other wildlife watching activities, it can be just as rewarding. Though amphibians and reptiles are masters at remaining unseen, patience, perseverance, some knowledge of the life history of species in the area and a bit of an adventurous spirit will allow you to observe and enjoy herpetiles on wild Delmarva.

"In the right light, at the right time, everything is extraordinary."

Aaron Rose

Atlantic Ocean coastal sand dune
(Preceding pages) Diamondback Terrapin
(Following pages) Atlantic Ocean beach

(Left) male and female Northern Cardinal · Scarlet Tanager · (Following pages) male Northern Cardinal

"There is a way
that nature speaks,
that land speaks.
Most of the time
we are simply not
patient enough,
quiet enough, to
pay attention to
the story."

-Linda Hogan

Pine Warbler • (Right) Common Yellowthroad • (Following pages) European Starling

(Left) female Red-winged Blackbird · male Red-winged Blackbird

(Left) Eastern Bluebird ◦ Indigo Bunting

"Like the resource it seeks to protect, wildlife conservation must be dynamic, changing as conditions change, seeking always to become more effective."

-*Rachel Carson*

(Preceeding pages and left) Great Blue Heron
(Following pages) Atlantic Ocean sunrise

THE SHIFTING SANDS OF ASSATEAGUE ISLAND

Derek Stoner
Derek Stoner is a lifelong outdoorsman who enjoys tracking, photographing and studying mammals. A naturalist for the Delaware Nature Society, he leads field trips in search of mammals and teaches the mammal course for the Naturalist Certification Series at Ashland Nature Center in Hockessin.

The low murmur of waves lapping the shoreline greets our band of visitors. Before us lays an expanse of sand, the piles of silica crystals deposited more than 3 feet deep atop the beach parking lot. Detritus cast from the ocean resembles the contents of a children's playhouse spilled upon the shore. Golden necklaces of Whelk eggs cling to wig-like masses of brown algae. Mounds of Lady Slippers, Razor Clams and Jingle Shells look like toddler toys cast aside.

It is November 2009, one week after a nor'easter and Hurricane Ida struck the beautiful barrier island of Assateague. The storm, which lasted two days, carved a path of destruction — and creation. Sand borne by powerful waves and fierce winds adds to the layers of material holding this fragile island in place.

Given time, the wind and the tides will rebuild the dune ecosystem that protects a barrier island. We are looking at a newborn ecosystem that is ready to grow and mature once again — only to be destroyed and rebuilt repeatedly.

Building a Barrier Island

From the air, the 36-mile Assateague Island resembles a curving needle laid along the southern end of the Delmarva Peninsula. Sitting off the Atlantic coast of Maryland and Virginia, Assateague — Native American for "a running stream between" — is bracketed by the Ocean City Inlet at the north end and Chincoteague Inlet at the southern terminus.

Assateague Island includes the Assateague Island National Seashore, run by the National Park Service. The Maryland portion of the island is also home to Assateague Island State Park. On the Virginia portion of the island is Chincoteague National Wildlife Reserve. Chincoteague Island, Virginia, located to the west, features the many tourist services that benefit from proximity to the parks and reserve.

Separated from the mainland by shallow bays, Assateague Island was formed from sediments eroded from the Appalachian Highlands to the west. These layers of soft sediments, now more than 8,000 feet thick, were deposited intermittently on the Atlantic Coastal Plain during periods of higher sea level over the past 100 million years.

Glaciers from the Pleistocene epoch during the ice age never reached southern Maryland, but periodic colder climates played a role in the formation of Assateague Island's landscape. During the ice age, sea level fluctuations caused the shorelines of the Atlantic barrier islands to migrate landward. At present, Assateague is migrating landward through a process called "island rollover." Sand is eroded from ocean beaches during severe storms, carried across the island by flood waters and redeposited in marshes along the western shore.

In 1933, a major hurricane slammed into the coast. The storm formed the Ocean City Inlet, separating Fenwick Island to the north and Assateague Island to the south. (Ocean City is on the end of Fenwick Island — which is not to be confused with the town Fenwick Island, Delaware, which is also on Fenwick Island.)

Since the inlet's creation, the Assateague shoreline has migrated westward more than 1,000 feet. In addition, a National Park Service study estimates that 6.6 million cubic meters of sand has relocated from Assateague Island due to the inlet's presence. An ambitious 25-year dredging project begun in 2002 seeks to replenish Assateague's beaches.

wild pony • (Following pages) Forster's Tern

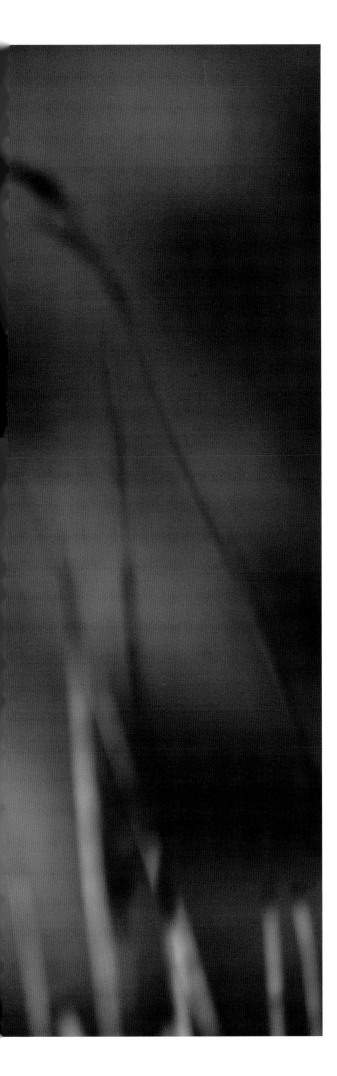

Preserving an Island Paradise

Human settlement on Assateague Island began in the early 1600s when members of the Nanticoke tribe (the Assateagues, Chincoteagues and Pocomokes) made camp on the island and took advantage of its bountiful natural resources. European colonization began in the late 1600s, and residents remained on the island into the 19th century, after which the federal government began buying up the land. The farming and grazing activities of the colonists created an unnatural landscape that may be seen today, especially if you view the island through a cultural historian's eye and spot the remnants of old barns and shacks.

In the past century, a series of forward-thinking efforts by the federal government helped preserve the natural beauty of Assateague Island. The Chincoteague National Wildlife Refuge was established at the southern end of the island in 1943 as a wintering area for migratory waterfowl. Today, the refuge includes more than 14,000 acres of beach, dunes, marsh and maritime forest, which provide habitat for waterfowl, wading birds, shorebirds and songbirds.

Due to the diversity of habitats and wildlife at Chincoteague, the United Nations has designated it a World Biosphere Reserve. The U.S. Department of the Interior has designated it a National Natural Landmark. According to the U.S. Fish & Wildlife Service, the Chincoteague National Wildlife Refuge each year receives about 1.4 million visits, making it one of the most visited refuges in the nation.

In the 1950s Assateague faced a new threat, as more than 5,000 lots on the island were zoned and sold for resort development. But the Ash Wednesday Storm of 1962 dashed those plans. In 1965, the National Park Service created the Assateague Island National Seashore. The park bustles year-round, drawing more than two million visitors, according to a 2008 report from the National Park Service.

In both cases, the visitor count may include people who came to the area more than once that year to enjoy the swimming, beachcombing, kayaking and birdwatching that the areas have to offer.

Bountiful Island Life

Vast expanses of salt marsh separate Assateague Island from the mainland, and nestled in between are the vibrant bays of Chincoteague and Sinepuxent. Renowned for their bounty of seafood, harvested by watermen and brought to tables all over the East Coast, these estuaries are a nursery for a multitude of life forms. The famous Chincoteague oysters are legendary among shellfish connoisseurs, possessing an extra-salty flavor imbued with a strong essence of their birthplace.

My introduction to the bustling bay biota came during a high school summer camp at the Marine Science Consortium in Wallops Island, Virginia. An entire week devoted to studying and literally immersing ourselves in coastal ecology made for an unforgettable adventure with new discoveries at every turn.

Aboard the wonderfully named RV Mollusk, our team of students set forth into the shallow waters of the Chincoteague Bay. Dropping a trawl behind the research vessel, we cruised a short distance before hauling in the net to inspect its squirming catch. Amidst the mats of marsh vegetation writhed a marine menagerie: Bay Anchovies, Silversides, Mummichogs, Oyster Toadfish, Flounders, Blue Crabs and a mishmash of mollusks.

The sharp-eyed instructor carefully pried a prize from the entangling embrace of eelgrass. It was a male Seahorse. An odd and un-scaled member of the fish family, the Seahorse is perfectly camouflaged to blend in with its sea grass habitat. The genus name of this amazing animal, Hippocampus, translates into "horse sea monster." While our wide-eyed group of teenagers saw no trace of monstrosity in the cute 3-inch-long Seahorse, we were

shocked to find such an exotic-looking creature living right here on our coast.

Years later, I come to Assateague with the vastly more-seasoned experience of a naturalist and still find an enchanting array of flora and fauna. Camera and binoculars in hand, I explore the island and continually discover new facets of Assateague. Perhaps the metaphor of the island as a rough diamond is apt; a sharp eye can find many ways to polish the place to sparkling brilliance. Time and patience will richly reward the Assateague explorer.

The "Big Three" animals on Assateague Island are the true mascots of this unique ecosystem: wild ponies, Sika Deer, and Delmarva Fox Squirrels. Given the island's status as a haven for visitors, it seems highly appropriate that all three are introduced species.

The history of wild ponies on Assateague is steeped in folklore and mystique. The popular legend holds that a Spanish galleon wrecked off the island, and the surviving ponies swam ashore. The more plausible theory is that early 17th century colonists let their animals loose on the island to graze freely. Either way, there is a tremendous sentimental attraction to these colorful horses, and few tourists leave Assateague without the requisite photos, postcards and memories of these magical equines.

More than 150 wild ponies now live on the Chincoteague National Wildlife Refuge. A fence divides Assateague in half, and the north section is home to another 150 ponies. Feeding off salt marsh grass, bayberry twigs and seaweed causes the ponies to drink twice as much fresh water as domestic horses, making them appear swollen and rotund.

Sika Deer emigrated from Japan in the 1920s, stocked on Assateague by an enterprising Boy Scout troop. A species of Asian elk, the deer are smaller than our native White-tailed Deer. Sikas sport a dark, reddish-brown coat dappled with white spots. A long way from their original homeland, the Sika Deer seem content grazing upon the salt-laden vegetation in the island marshes. Every fall, these tiny elk engage in their mating rituals, with the male stags bugling to attract the females —sort of scaled-down coastal version of our American elk performing in the western mountains.

The Delmarva Fox Squirrel is a true native of the Delmarva Peninsula but has a sad story. Loss of this squirrel's preferred open woodland habitat landed it on the federal endangered species list. Since squirrels are not accomplished swimmers, this species was brought to the Chincoteague refuge in 1968 as an introduction effort. Almost twice the size of a Gray Squirrel and possessing a much bushier tail, the Delmarva Fox Squirrel is a ghostly gray color. I seek them out along the Woodland Trail at Chincoteague, and I always marvel at how quietly they move about the loblolly pine forest. A pile of pinecone cuttings is a good clue that you've found the hangout of a Delmarva Fox Squirrel, and you might stay a while to watch the antics of this unique inhabitant of Delmarva.

Delmarva Fox Squirrel

If you are really lucky, you may even see the rare black morph Delmarva Fox Squirrel.

Not all the wonderful wildlife of Assateague is furry. Many folks flock to the island to view the feathered masses, with more than 300 species of birds occurring on the island throughout the year. More than 2,600 acres of shallow freshwater wetlands at Chincoteague are designed to attract waterbirds. Years ago I saw my first Redhead (a diving duck) while touring the refuge, and subsequent encounters with magnificent Peregrine Falcons, Bald Eagles, and Tundra Swans convinced me that this place is a birding paradise. Visit these impoundments in the fall and winter to witness the thousands of ducks, geese and swans. You'll have no reason to doubt why the National Audubon Society lists Assateague on its list of top 10 birding spots.

Return to the Storm Scene

The strong nor'easter in 2009 brought many surprises, with birds the most visible and eye-catching one of them. The storm not only deposited a load of sand on Assateague, but it also deposited a bundle of birds. During our November visit, a flock of White Ibis gathers near a sluice gate, slashing their blood-red curved beaks through the water with efficient strokes. Killifish, Mummichogs and minnows are snapped up into the White Ibises' mouths and gulped down their gullets.

The White Ibis is a bird commonly associated with the mangrove and cypress swamps of the Deep South, where they prey on shrimp and crawfish. A large flock of White Ibis appearing the week before Thanksgiving in northern Virginia is a sign of Mother Nature's penchant to sweep up avian cargo during her tempests and deposit these birds in far-flung places.

As we wandered along the strand, we spotted a small bird battling its way against a strong headwind. Careful scrutiny identified this winged wonder as a Cave Swallow, a species normally found in Texas and New Mexico. Storm systems bring vagrant Cave Swallows to the east each fall, where they follow the coast back south. We wished this tiny swallow well as it journeyed back to wintering grounds in Mexico.

From far and wide, Assateague collects visitors of all types: human, plant and animal. On the edge of the most densely populated region in the United States, you can lose yourself in the peaceful scenery and relaxing atmosphere of Assateague Island. Whether you stake out a beach umbrella amidst the throngs of tourists, hike the woodlands in search of songbirds, or cruise the roads on pony patrol, you will likely find Assateague Island is nothing if not a generous host towards gracious visitors.

Great Blue Heron
(Following pages) frozen Lewes, Delaware beach

(Preceding pages) Cape Henlopen State Park, Lewes, Delaware after a storm   •   (Left) Bay Scallop   •   Welk shell

"The most unhappy
thing about conservation is
that it is never permanent.
If we save a priceless

Harp Seal

woodland today, it is
threatened from another

quarter tomorrow."

-Marjory Stoneman Douglas

(left) Gray Seal   •   (Following four pages) World War II fire
control towers on Delaware's Atlantic coast

"The World we all
share is given to us
in trust. Every choice
we make regarding
the earth, air, and
water around us
should be made
with the objective
of preserving it for
all generations
to come."

-August A. Bush III

(Preceding pages) Black Skimmer and
Snowy Egrets • Ring-billed Gull

"There are some who can live without wild things, and some who cannot. ...Like winds and sunsets, wild things were taken for granted until progress began to do away with them. Now we face the question whether a still higher 'standard of living' is worth its cost in things natural, wild, and free. For us of the minority, the opportunity to see geese is a right as inalienable as free speech."

-Aldo Leopold

Northern Gannet

"The more clearly
we can focus our
attention on
the wonders
and realities of
the universe,
the less taste we
shall have for
destruction."

-*Rachel Carson*

(Left and above) Black-necked Stilt • (Following pages) Double-crested Cormorant chicks

Double-crested Cormorant playing with Magnolia cone

Double-crested Cormorant chick • (Following pages) Striped Bass

Blue Crab

"For if one link
in nature's chain
might be lost,
another might
be lost, until the
whole of things
will vanish
piecemeal."

-Thomas Jefferson

Snowy Egrets

Snowy Egret

(Left and above) Snowy Egrets fighting

Snowy Egrets fighting

"Without habitat, there is no wildlife. It is that simple."

-Wildlife Habitat Canada

Snowy Egret and Forster's Tern   •   (Following pages) Raccon family

"How can any child who is unfamiliar with the animals, birds, plants, insects, rocks, soils and water of their own home neighborhood, develop into a progressive citizen with respect to the proper use of these resources?"

-Alice Hall Walter

young Raccoon

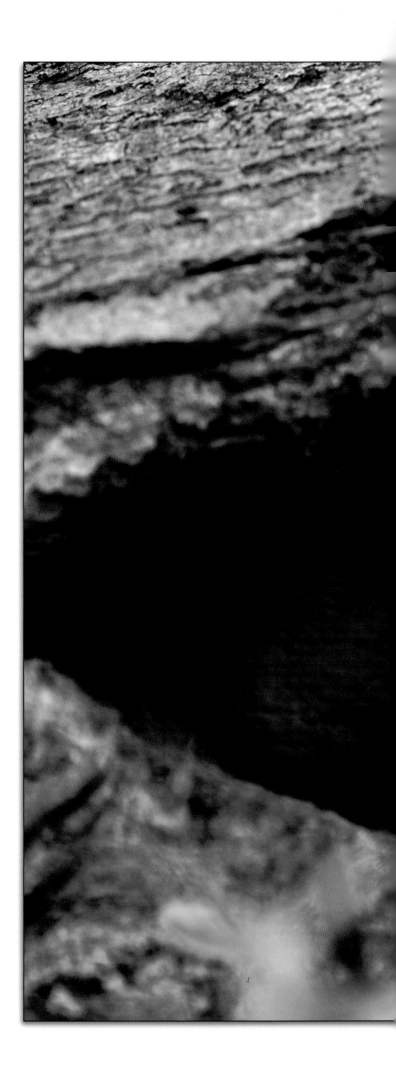

Red Fox kit

(Left) Red Fox kit with European Starling   •   Red Fox

(Above and right) Red Fox kits

(Following pages) Wild Turkey

"How rich will
we be when we
have converted
all our forests,
our soil, our
water resources,
and our minerals
into cash?"

-Jay Norwood "Ding" Darling

"I recognize the
right and duty of
this generation to
develop and use
the natural resources
but I do not
recognize the right
to waste them or to
rob, by wasteful use,
the generations that
come after us."

-Theodore Roosevelt

Lesser Yellowlegs

(Above and following pages) Black-crowned Night Heron

"Nature never

goes out of style."

-author unknown

young Black-Crowned Night Heron   •   (Right) American Bittern

"The continued existence of wildlife and wilderness is important to the quality of life of humans."

-Jim Fowler

Clapper Rail

Royal Tern

(Above and following pages) Royal Terns

"Conservation... is a positive exercise of skill and insight, not merely a negative exercise of abstinence and caution..."

-Aldo Leopold

Belted Kingfisher

"I'm learning one thing the hard way... you have to re-educate the public mind about conservation every 15 or 20 years or it forgets everything learned a while back."

-Jay Norwood "Ding" Darling

(Preceeding, left and following four pages) Northern Pintail

"We owe it to our children to be better stewards of the environment. The alternative? A world without whales. It's too terrible to imagine."

-Pierce Brosnan

(Preceding four pages) frozen Mispillion River
(Preceeding pages) Herring Point,
Cape Henlopen State Park

(Above and following pages) Minke Whale bones and skull

(Left and above) Tricolored Heron • (Following pages) Great Blue Heron

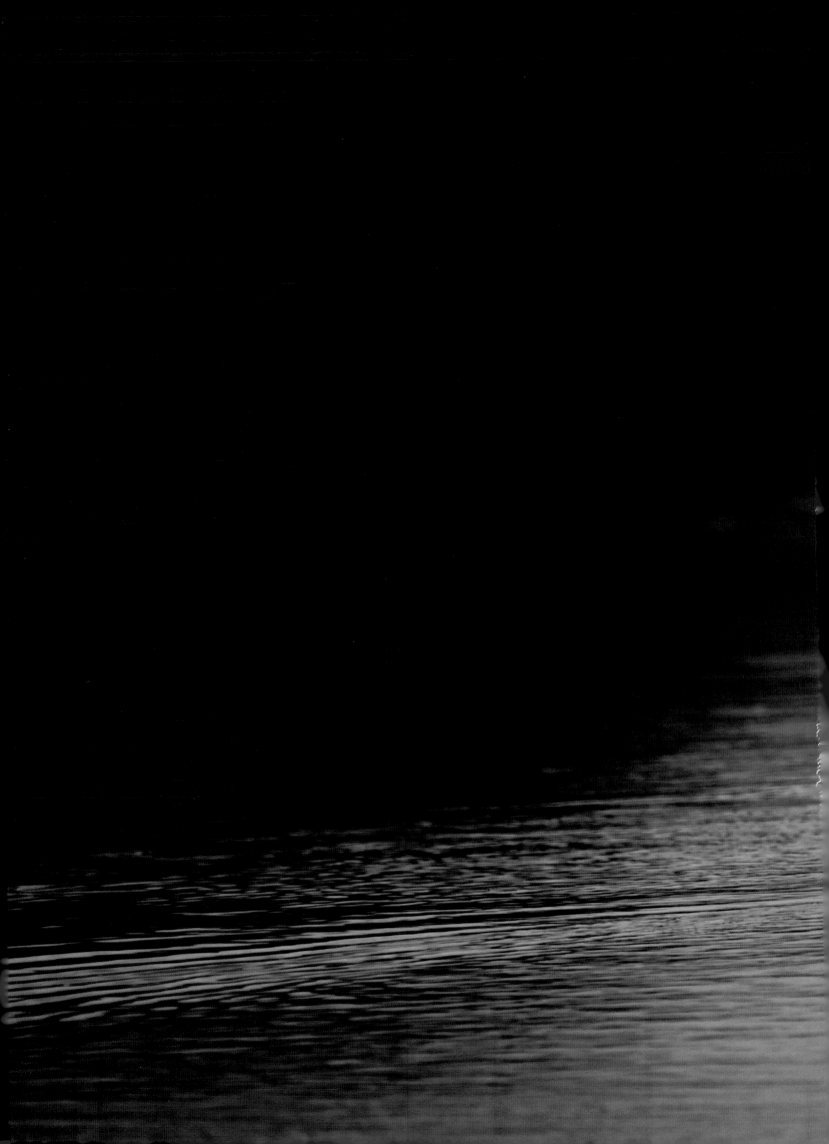